The *Secret* Agent

The Secret *Daily System for Amazing Success--*

Leverage the Awesome Powers of the Movie *The Secret!*

And Go Several Steps Beyond… to

Transform Your Business and Brighten Your Life!

by Ralph Merritt Nedelkoff

Copyright 2008 by Ralph M. Nedelkoff
All Rights Reserved

Cover Design by Alan Kobayashi

Note: This book is about some of the principles in the 2006 documentary video and DVD *The Secret*, copyright TS Production LLC, and the similar teachings of the 1986 audio CD *The Strangest Secret* by Earl Nightingale, copyright Nightingale Conant Corp., and some additional principles that go beyond those in the movie and the audio book. This book and its author are not in any way associated with the movie *The Secret,* its author or its production company TS Production LLC, and this book and its author are not in any way associated with *The Strangest Secret* and its author. This book is also about some of the teachings of dozens of other speakers and authors who have been teaching the principles of *The Secret* and *The Strangest Secret* over the past three decades. This book is also based upon the original concepts, teachings and systems of the author of this book based upon many personal and professional experiences and observations. The opinions expressed in this book are solely those of its author.

Contents

Dedication --- Page 3

Important Preface and Acknowledgement --- Page 4

Section One: What is the Awesome Power of *The Secret?* Go Beyond The Secret to Live a Powerful Daily System that will Utterly Transform Your Life? --- Page 6

Section Two: How Can *You* Absolutely Assure Your Success in Real Estate Sales? Why Do Most People Flounder or Fail? --- Page 10

Section Three: How You Empower *The Secret* and Beyond in Your Life! --Follow this System and Take these Action Steps to Create and Build a Brighter Life! --- Page 13

Section Four: What Could Hold Us Back or Encourage Breakdowns? --- Page 31

Section Five: How You Get Your Big Mo Magic Going! --Follow the System with Fun Daily Action Steps --- Page 33

Section Six: A Summary of the Important Steps to Attract Your Success and Happiness --- Page 36

Section Seven: Create Your Vision Book --- Page 39

Section Eight: A Framework for Focus -- A Framework for Your Yearly, Monthly and Weekly Business Plans --- Page 50

Section Nine: My Daily Vision Sheets --- Page 56

About the Author --- Page 60

Dedication

    This book—this action book—is dedicated to *everyone* with big dreams. To *anyone* who aspires for personal improvement and a higher level of success and happiness in life. It is also very powerful for someone in the extremely challenging but potentially highly lucrative and satisfying field of real estate sales, marketing and consulting. And for everyone who aspires to a brighter, happier, more fulfilling life and is willing take the initiative to attract it.

    Whatever you want… If you focus on it, believe it, have faith and live it in a daily system, you will attract into your life. Anything you want.

    Life is short. Life can be fun and fulfilling and rewarding. Your life can be truly amazing! You can make it even more amazing. Transform your life! Attract everything you really desire. Take these first steps! And *enjoy* the journey!

-- Ralph Merritt Nedelkoff

Important Preface and Acknowledgement

The wonderful 2006 video and DVD *The Secret* by TS Production LLC became one of the most popular DVD's of the year. Among millions of personal development devotees, mainly through their word of mouth, it became a widespread cultural classic. Before that, Earl Nightingale recorded an audio book called *The Strangest Secret* on the very same principle and it has been popular for decades.

One of the beauties of the video is that it makes *The Secret* of success in life so simple. It reveals "The Secret of the Universe." It shows how it has been passed on throughout history. It offers the viewer three simple steps to attract success: Ask, Believe, then Receive. In a complex world, it is wonderful that *The Secret* simplifies the essence of attracting success and happiness. This is a good thing. It enlightens us and really drives home the main point. And if you do it, it works!

However, we live complex personal lives and complex business lives. Most individuals need a lot more structure and a lot more detailed process than simply: Ask, Believe, then Receive. Individuals yearn for a much more structured process—a system—that they can use and personalize to *their* dreams, *their* lives, *their* situations and *their* business—to implement and leverage the amazing powers of *The Secret* on a daily and consistent basis. That is the purpose of this action book.

Some of us are afraid to dream big. Many of us have big dreams—we know what we want—but these big dreams just don't come true in our lives. We know vaguely what we want to do in our lives and our careers, but somehow, it just doesn't get done. Or at least, it doesn't get done to the level we want. Why? There are many reasons. The most powerful reasons are: We are not applying the powers of *The Secret* in our lives. But we need more than that. We need to go beyond *The Secret*. We need a lot more details, and the structure and the system to apply them.

This book both embellishes upon and also goes far beyond the three critical but somewhat vague principles of Ask, Believe and Receive. It has been proven that it is absolutely essential to Ask, Believe and Receive. However, we also need to take constructive action on a daily basis in our businesses and our lives. This is how we thrive! This is how we maximize our lives!

This action book offers you the detailed answers and provides for you the detailed framework and format in response to the questions: "Okay, I've seen the movie. I loved it. It's fantastic! I want to live *The Secret*. I want to harness the awesome powers of the universe in my life and my business. *Now*, what do I do? What steps do I take next?"

This action book—and it is a *action book*—is for you to actually use, and use daily—not just read once and cast aside. This book offers you a valuable and practical system—that you can personalize to *your* dreams, *your* life, *your* situation and *your* business, and implement the powers of *The Secret* on a daily and consistent basis.

You probably already know from your experience that simply watching a video and reading a book may be entertaining *and* educational, but it may not benefit or change your life. The only way you will really change your life is to actually put into practice on a systematic, daily basis what you have learned and have been inspired to do. Changing your life, improving your life, and improving your business all require *focused action* on a daily basis. *Your focused action!*

Yes, your dreams definitely can come true! Yes, the awesome powers of *The Secret* are true! Yes, *The Secret* can change your life! Yes, *The Secret* can dramatically improve your business and career! But YOU need to take the first steps and make a true personal commitment to actually *use* this action book!

Go ahead. Do it now! Grab a pen or pencil, go to a table or desk and let's get started! Attract your success!

Section One

What is the Awesome Power of *The Secret*?
Go beyond The Secret to Live a Powerful Daily System that will Utterly Transform Your Life!

As you may know, the 2006 video *The Secret* became a bit of a sub-cultural phenomenon among millions of personal development devotees. It is based upon the books and teachings of dozens of leading scientists, philosophers, personal development trainers and motivational speakers. It is also based upon myths, ancient legends, and various religious and philosophical teachings throughout the centuries.

The *Secret* attributes the amazing success of some of the most remarkable people throughout history to their knowing and practicing the *The Secret -- The Great Secret of the Universe.* It claims that research has shown us that many of the greatest people throughout history such as Plato, Newton, Carnegie, Beethoven, Shakespeare, Franklin, Lincoln, Whitman, Einstein, Bell, Edison and many others understood and lived *The Secret. The Secret* dramatically transformed their lives and the lives of all those who lived it.

What is *The Secret? The Secret* quite simply is the Law of Attraction. The basic principle that *everything we focus on, we attractive into our lives. We attract into our lives that which we think about, envision and believe.* This has been proven again and again throughout history.

Again: *everything we focus on, whether it is good, bad, positive, negative, disastrous or truly amazing and wonderful, we attractive into our lives.* We attract into our lives that which we think about, envision and firmly believe.

Think about it…and you will know that it is true.

The Secret applies to all facets of our lives. It applies to our joy, health, happiness, relaxation, love, relationships, jobs, businesses, prosperity, wealth and achievement. Why do some people attract joy and happiness and others attract misery? Why do some people attract stress and anxiety and others attract peace and relaxation. Why do some people attract wonderful health and fitness and others attract unfitness and frequent illness? Why do some people attract love and others attract hatred? Why do some people attract positive vibrations and others attract negative vibrations? Why do some people attract wealth and abundance and others attract poverty and scarcity? Why are some people energized and others are lethargic? Why are some people generally successful and others chronic failures? Why are some people in a great mood while others are sad and depressed? Why are some people self-limited and self-repressed and others let their dreams and spirit soar?

The ultimate answer is *The Secret*. If we analyze each specific situation in regard to ourselves and other people we know very well, and we consider each situation honestly and objectively, we will likely come to the insightful conclusion: We attract it all into our lives. What ever it is, we attract it. Our dreams, visions, focus, beliefs and actions determine what we become.

In regard to personal achievement in our lives: That which we completely desire, focus on, believe in and act upon, we will achieve. However, it takes a tested and systematic approach to take our vague personal dreams to complete, successful fruition. Our personal success and achievement is always a process. And for higher degrees of personal success and achievement, our process needs to be a tested and systematic process. The more systematic and fine-tuned our process for personal achievement, the quicker and easier it will become for us. And, the more success we will achieve. The process will become much more *fun* and much more *rewarding!*

Have you ever noticed how some people with wishes and desires always seem to struggle? They don't know exactly what they want in life. They drift a little, they try, they fail, they try something else, they succeed a little, they fail, they try something else, they succeed a little and they fail. They continually get down and discouraged, try again, get discouraged, and so on and so on. Then they come to some unfortunate conclusions: Life's a bear! Life is unfair! Why is everyone else doing so well and I'm not? They are no better than me! Why am I always in a rut and other people are soaring? Why am *I* struggling and *they* seem to make everything look easy? Why are *they* so lucky? Why do *I* always seem to have bad luck? *Why me?* they ask. Unfortunately, they just don't have a clue. Why? Why?

You guessed it. *The Secret.*

Why not cut out the misery? Simply embrace *The Secret!* Live *The Secret!* Learn to harness its awesome power! Let your inner spirit soar!

To really harness its power, you must learn to develop it, embellish it and fine-tune it and put it into a functional and highly effective daily system. Many people, after having seen the video *The Secret* and having been very impressed with it, have commented: "It seems so simple—maybe a bit too hocus-pocus. You mean all I have to do is wish for something and I'll get it? My wish—the Genie's command?"

No. Its instructions to apply *The Secret* were a little more detailed than that. But still not detailed enough—especially in regard to attracting much more success into your complex business life and your hectic personal life. You may try to simply dream something, wait for the universe to attract it and achieve success as implied in the movie. But to take your business to a much higher level, it takes a much more detailed process. Simply wishing and hoping is not enough. To take your entire life to a much higher level of happiness and fulfillment, if not bliss—and to *assure* your success, you will need to follow a proven system and create powerful new daily habits. You need to take important *daily actions* that are totally in alignment with the achievement of your hopes, dreams and visions! This requires a proven method and a fun, highly functional system. These methods and systems have worked in some amazing ways for others, and they will work for you. You just have to learn the precise methods and systems that will work for you through a *process of self-discovery.* Then *adapt* them to your individual situation. Then *adopt* them! Then *do* them! Take action daily! If you implement the critical details of this system and this process, you will *know* what you really want in life. And you *will achieve* exactly what you want in life: Just dream it, visualize it, believe it and do it! And use this system!

This book goes far beyond *The Secret* and *The Strangest Secret*. It gives you the structure and system to work *The Secret* daily, and to create amazing weeks and months and years ahead of you. It is your detailed road map for your exciting, empowering journey. Let's check out the actual specifics necessary to help empower you…and to brighten if not utterly transform your life!

Let's start the fun! Expect to change your life!!!

Section Two

How Can *You* Absolutely Assure Your Success in Real Estate Sales? Why Do Most People Flounder or Fail?

News flash: The statistics are in. Although we see many exciting success stories throughout the business, most individuals who attempt a career in residential real estate sales and marketing fail and drop out of the business or flounder terribly. And it is the overwhelmingly vast majority that fail or flounder. At various times and places approximately 60% will fail or flounder. At other times and places approximately 90% will fail or flounder. Most experts will agree that the average failure rate runs at approximately 80%. It's old 80/20 Rule, sometimes known as Pareto's Principle. In regard to real estate sales, it is the principle that approximately 20% of the real estate agents make 80% of the money, and that 80% fail or flounder and 20% succeed or prosper. The exact statistics vary from time to time and place to place depending on such factors as the strength of the real estate market, the strength of the local economy, the competitiveness of the local market, the consumer confidence in the local market, the training of the agent, the knowledge of the agent, the personal finances of the agent needed to run a business, the dedication and commitment of the agent, the personality and abilities of the agent, the motivation of the agent, and *most importantly—the mindset and the daily habits of the agent!* When an agent falls short of success in any kind of market, experience has shown that the most critical factors are the *agent's mindset and daily habits.* These struggling and failing agents seem to attract failure and misery, rather that fulfillment and success. And unfortunately, many of these individuals don't really know why.

"What's the answer? What's the solution? What will work in any kind of market? What is the real secret to success?" you may ask. Of course, it is learning, believing in and implementing daily the powerful principles of *The Secret.*

This powerful process is the foundation for every success in your life. Look at the winners—look at the losers, now and through time. What will you discover? What will you learn? What will you learn from their successes? What will you learn from their failures? What are the important lessons?

Answer: Without the foundation of this powerful process, your success will almost certainly become much more of a struggle, much more sporadic, much more limited and maybe even doomed to ultimate failure. And by utilizing this powerful process, *anything* you can imagine—*anything* you can vividly envision, believe in and act upon, you can achieve! Your possibilities are boundless and unlimited. Your dreams can be unfettered! You will live a powerful and fulfilling life! Your ultimate dreams *will* be fulfilled!

Is this all something miraculous and unexplained? Is this all hocus-pocus stuff? Well, the movie actually does make the process seem a bit magical, mysterious and effortless. But the principles of *The Secret* and the similar teachings of thousands of scientist, psychologists, philosophers, personal performance trainers and motivational speakers are based upon proven facts. The biggest and most important fact is: This system works!!! It has been proven again and again. This is how our minds work!!! We attract what we ask for, focus on and believe. And, taking it one step further, we attract what we act upon!

These powerful principles are alluded to in the Bible and the teachings of many religions. Reverend Robert H. Schuller and his son, in their television sermons, and others have espoused these very principles and have written many books about them for decades. Reverend Joel Osteen has become popular teaching these principles. Dr. Wayne Dyer and many others have written and spoken on these principles. Anthony Robbins has created a huge personal performance enhancement empire weaving in these important principles. And Jack Canfield and Mark Victor Hansen have sold well over 100 million books actually having utilized these principles and also having taught them. Even Donald Trump has co-written a book on the subject—obviously attempting to supplement his meager income from his signature filet mignon business. But seriously, millions of people have achieved health, wealth, happiness and enormous personal success by learning, believing and implementing these powerful principles.

Warning: This is a system that requires possibility thinking. It requires faith! And to achieve true success with it, you will need a detailed, systematic process to follow on a daily basis. If you feel that you are too busy to implement these systems, that is a limiting belief. You might as well stop right now—until you change your attitude.

Warning: Reading this book is not enough! You must take action and do the exercises in this book! This powerful system requires a true personal commitment to use some time to do the exercises each day—generally 5 to 20 minutes. It's like exercising. You can't lose weight and get in shape by only reading about it! You make the commitment, schedule the time, take action each day, and soon it becomes an enjoyable and fulfilling habit with wonderful results you desire.

If you feel your life is perfect already and you don't desire any self-improvement, you might as well stop right now. We all know, half-hearted efforts seldom succeed; so don't waste your precious time.

If you really don't have any as yet unfulfilled dreams or desires, then end it now. If you do not aspire to greater health, happiness, prosperity and personal fulfillment, you might as well go take a nap or read another book. This is a system for people who want more in lives than they have now. And are willing to make a relatively small, but hugely significant commitment each day. This is for individuals who want to flourish! This is for individuals who want to live a *magnificent life!*

Think about what it would mean to you and your life and the lives of your loved ones if you were to utterly transform your life and your career, and achieve your full, amazing potential for joy, health, wealth and happiness.

Got bliss? Got business? Got money? Or need more of it? Then keep reading!

Section Three

How You Empower *The Secret* in Your Life!
--Follow this System and Take these Action Steps to Create and Build a Brighter Life!

The *Secret* is the Law of Attraction: We attract into our lives that which we think about, envision and firmly believe. Believe it!

This has been proven again and again throughout history. It will work for YOU! Take action daily! Use this system to brighten your life!

The movie, *The Secret* is applied to your life daily in three simple steps:
1. Ask—for exactly what you want
2. Believe and Visualize—that it will happen and the universe will attract it
3. Receive—it when it comes to you

However, to really make the process much more powerful and highly effective in regard to your life and your business, you will need to take *more* steps, go into a lot *more* details, and you will need to implement it in a *daily system*. And before you implement the system, you will have to personalize it to your personal needs, desires and your personal situation. To do this, you must ask yourself some very important questions and write down your responses in some key actions steps.

*First: ASK
Ask for exactly what you want in a voice as if you have already received it. Write it and say it out loud. And do it with an attitude of gratitude! Begin each day in

gratitude. Live each day in gratitude. Ask for exactly what you want in a statement of gratitude.

Examples: "I am so happy and grateful now that I have made over $500,000 in income." "I am so happy and grateful now that I have acquired a terrific five million dollar buyer." "I am so happy and grateful now that I have acquired a terrific three million dollar seller."

"I am so happy and grateful that I could help my wonderful buyers get the home of their dreams and make them happy!"

"I am so happy and grateful now that I have made _____ sales this month."

"I am so happy and grateful for my energy and my health."

Ask for whatever is significant to you no matter how big or small. Express your true desires! Take the time to do it right now. Go ahead:

"I am so happy and grateful now that... _____
_____
_____"

"I am so happy and grateful for... _____
_____"

"I am so happy and grateful now that... _____
_____
_____"

"I am so happy and grateful for... _____
_____"

"I am so happy and grateful now that... _____
_____
_____"

"I am so happy and grateful for... _____
_____"

"I am so happy and grateful now that… _____

_____

_____ ,,

"I am so happy and grateful for… _____

_____ ,,

_____

"I am so happy and grateful now that… _____

_____

_____ ,,

"I am so happy and grateful for… _____

_____ ,,

_____

*Second: BELIEVE

Believe that it will happen and the universe will attract it.

Believe it by visualizing and feeling the end result. Know it will happen. Trust the universe. Have faith!

Use verbal incantations. Say them out loud! Believe your words. Create your words! Create you beliefs:

"Money comes to me easily and frequently."

"I always attract what I desire!"

"I enjoy my work!"

"I love this business!"

"I love all the wonderful opportunities available to me!"

"I seize my opportunities!"

"I enjoy making $_____ per year!"

"I enjoy attaining $_____ million in net worth!"

"I create my fantastic life!"

"I plan my success!"

"I work my plan daily!"

The Secret Agent—The Secret Daily System for Amazing Success

"I am unstoppable!

"I create my success!"

"I love to create abundance!"

"I love to help others!"

Write down several beliefs:

_____
_____
_____
_____
_____
_____
_____
_____
_____
_____
_____
_____
_____
_____
_____

*Third: VISUALIZE

Visualize it as if it has happened.

Create your personal VISION and YOUR VISION BOOK

Create a brief list of your deepest personal desires—your passions. Take a few moments to self-discover what is MOST important to you and your happiness.

Jot down some brief responses. Be honest with yourself. If you are not honest, the system just won't work. For example, if you say that you want to make a million dollars a year, but when it comes down to reality, you would be very happy making $90,000 and enjoying other things in your life, then it is the $90,000 that is most important to you, not the million. A lot of people would say that they would like to make a million dollars a year, but is that what is most important to them? Most likely not! That's why they don't make the million dollars. They fall way short. It was a fanciful wish, but it was not really that important to them. But if *you* really, really desire to make the million dollars, then don't sell yourself short! You can do it! Remember *The Secret* – We attract that which we focus on, envision and believe. Ask yourself:

- What do I really want in my life? What is most important?

_____
_____
_____
_____
_____
_____

- What do I really want to achieve most?

_____
_____
_____
_____
_____
_____

- What do I really want to attain most?

_____
_____
_____

- What do I really want to obtain most?

_____

- What do I most want to do for myself and for others?

_____

Stop and think about yourself. Be genuine, authentic and honest. Decide what *you really* want, not what you think you *should want*. And not what *others* think you should want. It's *your* life, not theirs! Living someone else's agenda could become quite stressful. Be yourself. Be happy!

Don't be afraid to dream big! But be real with yourself. You will now need to ask yourself several more important personal questions. The first critical question will help you discover your big "Why?" in life. You will discover the most powerful motivations in your life. Without strong, extremely powerful and vivid motives, you will drift, flounder and continually fall short of attaining your dreams and desires.

First, ask: What really motivates me?

Is it a desire to make more money? If so, what specifically would I do with the additional money that would make me happier? Would I buy a new car? If so, exactly what kind of car? Would it be a brand new white Mercedes SL 600 sport luxury sedan with tan interior? Whatever it is, find a color photo of that exact car, cut it out and paste it in your Vision Book in Section Seven of this action book. Would it be a Hawaiian vacation? Then cut out a gorgeous color photo of the beach in Hawaii and paste it in your Vision Book! Would you invest in putting your kids through college? Then paste in a photo or logo of a college. Want to achieve $5 million in net assets? Then white out the total in your bank account or investment account statement and type in $5,872,536 or whatever. Or find a photo of piles of money and paste it in your book. If you want to buy 8 investment properties, paste in photos of 8 investment properties. If you want to buy a new dream home for yourself, paste in a photo of the home of your dreams. You get the idea. Find your passions! Just do it!

Or is your primary motivator a desire for prestige? Is it your pride and your enjoyment of striving for the highest standards of excellence? Is it your competitive nature—always going for #1? Is it getting acknowledgement and awards for your accomplishments? If so, then paste in a photo of the type of award plaque you would like to achieve, or write an exact description of the award you want. Would it be #3 in your office or #2 or # 1? Would it be the acknowledgement for achieving $20 million in sales or $50 million or more? What would you be passionate about?

Is your motivation a sheer passion for the business and a total enjoyment of your daily business activities? If so, then paste in photos of some of the properties you are selling or have sold. Or photos of your office or some of your happy clients.

Is it the dream of a better life for your family that motivates and inspires you? Then add photos of your family members into your Vision Book.

Is it a sense of mission to help other people and the satisfaction derived from that? Add photos of your clients.

The Secret Agent—The Secret Daily System for Amazing Success

Is your true passion making a lot of money so you can give it away to charity? Exactly which charity will you support and how much money will you donate. Write it all in your Vision Book and look at it daily.

In the real estate business, there are no correct answers as to what are the best motivators for top agents. Each individual is unique and many have different motivating influences. However, one motivator is almost universally in the top three for the highest achieving agents. It is the true sense of mission to serve their clients with the highest quality of service. Each agent who has excelled in the real estate sales business over a long, successful career has been motivated by the desire to help their clients in any way possible, and not *just* chase business. If you do not have a strong sense of duty to your clients you may have some short-term success, but you will not get repeat business or referrals.

Building a career and making very good money are powerful motivators for most successful agents, but not necessarily all. There are quite a few successful agents involved in real estate sales who are quite wealthy—from their earnings, their spouse's earnings or inherited wealth—and these agents do not really *have* to work. They work hard and continue to excel, motivated primarily by a sense of pride in accomplishment and by the sheer joy of the work.

If making more money is one of your prime motivators, make sure you write down very specifically what amount of money you desire to make and by when. And write down exactly what you would spend it on and invest it in. Then, write how this additional money will make you happier. How would it change your life or your family's lifestyle? If a major motivator you listed is family, what exactly do you want to do with your family or for your family? If one is pride in achievement, what exactly do you want to achieve? In other words, take the time to discover your big "Why's." Your mission and purpose in life. Why will you wake up and get to work? Why will you take the initiative and invest the hours of your time necessary to build your real estate business? Know exactly what motivates you and remind yourself of it on a daily basis. See your bright light. Move towards it!

The Secret Agent—The Secret Daily System for Amazing Success

Write down your top two or three motivations in detail and rank them in order of importance. Write the exact details of why it will motivate you and exactly what your life will look like when you achieve it. If you are not keenly aware of what in your life passionately motivates you, and if you do not remind yourself constantly—you simply will not be motivated. The more motivated you are—the more successful you will be. The more motivated and successful you are—the more true joy and satisfaction you will experience in your life.

Examples:

1. My top motivator is to make a lot more money this coming year. I will earn $400,000 in the next 12 months. I will add $30,000 to Jason's college fund and $30,000 to Amanda's college fund. We will take and enjoy a one-week family ski vacation at Lake Tahoe in late February and a one-week family vacation in Washington, DC and Williamsburg in mid August. I will invest $24,000 of my earnings, or $2,000/mo. in stocks and mutual funds in the next 12 months. I will invest $85,000 of my earnings in money market funds and CD's to add to our savings for the down payment for a $750,000 new brick 4 bedroom 2.5 bath ranch home with a pool in the Silver Crest area that we will purchase within 11 months. I will trade in my 3 year old leased Ford Focus for a brand new navy blue Jaguar XJ with tan leather interior on June 14th. I will invest in a powerful new Toshiba laptop computer immediately after my next closing. I will donate $12,000 to children's cancer research this year.

2. My second motivator is pride in achievement. I will achieve the Most Improved Real Estate Agent in my company award over the next 12 months. I can just see myself receiving the award at our annual award ceremony. It will make me feel great! I will build my business up to be in the top 10% of agents in my office. I will be one of the top producers and leaders in my office. Within 30 days I will achieve and attain the prestigious designation of Certified Luxury Properties Consultant or CLPC from the Association of

Luxury Properties Consultants and TheWorldOfLuxuryRealEstate.com I am truly committed to all of these accomplishments and will be very proud of each of these accomplishments. I will feel fantastic!!!

Now, take the time to do yours. This is fun! Do it now!

My Top 3 Motivators and Why:

1. _____

2. _____

3. _____

Second, ask: How much money do I want to make in the next five years? Set your personal goal. Think big! You can do it. And write it down. You will refer to it constantly.

I will earn a total of $ _____ over the next five years.

Third, ask: What are the necessary personal characteristics and qualities I must manifest in order to accomplish my plan? What kind of a person do I need to be? How will I need to act in order to excel? Write down at least three personal characteristics. You will remind yourself of them constantly.

_____
_____
_____
_____
_____
_____
_____
_____
_____
_____
_____
_____
_____
_____
_____
_____
_____

Fourth, ask: Which fellow real estate agent do I admire most and why? We all look to role models to learn from and to inspire us. It is a part of human nature. Find someone excellent in your local area you can model to some extent.

My Role Model: _____

Why:_____

_____

Fifth, ask: What will be my main sources of finding buyers? List at least four or five.

Sixth, ask: What will be my main sources of finding sellers? List at least four or five.

Seventh, ask: What excites me most about this business? What do you love about it? Either make a list of what excites you, or write several paragraphs about your passions in your own words. You will refer to it constantly.

Eighth, ask: Where do you see yourself in five years? Dream big! Write a very detailed description of your future and the lifestyle you will enjoy. Write about what will be your stature in your real estate community in five years.

_____
_____
_____
_____
_____
_____
_____
_____

Congratulations! You have just created your VISION—of yourself and your future. Remember to refer to your personal written vision of your future often and review it on a consistent basis. Your VISION will motivate you and inspire you to take the actions that are necessary to fulfill your dreams.

You must clearly *envision* your success in order to *attract* your success…and *achieve* your success.

Make sure to schedule some time to find photos and cutouts that match your personal dreams and desires and motivations and paste them in your Vision Book in Section Seven of this action book.

*Fourth: RECEIVE:

Be ready and open to receive what you want. Visualize it. Feel it. Look for it. Accept it. It will happen. Feel the way you will once it arrives. Enjoy the feeling. Accept it when it arrives. Step into your successful future. Act as if it is happening all the time. Receive each and every thing you have asked for and have visualized having in your life. Relax and receive. And enjoy receiving! All that you want, ask for, believe in and act upon is yours! Visualize receiving it. *Feel* that you are receiving it. You deserve it! You have received it. Enjoy!

The Secret Agent—The Secret Daily System for Amazing Success

*Fifth: ACT!

This step goes beyond *The Secret*. Look for opportunities. Awaken to recognize opportunities. Expect opportunities to arise. Make opportunities arise. Attract them. Seize opportunities daily! Action is essential to success! Time is of the essence daily. Write down your written commitments. Schedule each commitment. Step into your visions! Make decisions to act! Take action with passion! Achieve each commitment. Just do it! Do it daily! It is essential to take action! Take productive action daily!

*Sixth: Live each day in GRATITUDE:

Develop a powerful attitude of gratitude. Begin each day by being grateful! Create a list daily of what you are grateful for in your life. And end each day in gratitude. The greatest antidote for fear, anxiety and stress is your expression of gratitude. When things go well and as you desire, be grateful for your wonderful gifts and successes. When things go not as well and not as you desire, be grateful for what you have in your life. Appreciate everything good that comes into your life. Be grateful and express it daily.

Repeat incantations of gratitude.

Examples: "I am so grateful for…" "I love my life!" "I love myself." "I love my opportunities!" I am so grateful for…"

Make your gratitude list. Write it now!

1. _____
_____
2. _____
_____
3. _____
_____
4. _____
_____

5. _____
_____
6. _____
_____
7. _____
_____
8. _____
_____
9. _____
_____
10. _____
_____

Now didn't that feel great! Feeling and expressing gratitude empowers us to deal successfully with the so-called or perceived ups and downs of daily life. Gratitude helps to bring peace into our lives.

Expressing gratitude will allow you to put your ups and downs in perspective. Many of the most highly successful and happy individuals in the world are those who deal best with their so-called failures. Our failures are nothing more that temporary setbacks and new challenges. Everyone has many setbacks and challenges. It is not the event, but your perception of the event and your reaction to it that are most important. It is how you perceive and react to each setback or each new challenge that will ultimately determine your success. Some people will view a major setback as a major life-changing disaster. Others will use the very same major setback as a launch pad for the most amazing life-changing successes.

The most highly successful individuals see setbacks as insignificant and only temporary. They see them as useful learning experiences that allow them to fine-tune their strategies and actions. They do not dwell on them and revel in misery.

They do not perceive problems as bad luck and setbacks as disasters. Setbacks are merely empowering challenges and are a necessary part of navigating through life.

Successful individuals see challenges as strengthening and empowering opportunities. They strive for success. They visualize success. They attract success!

You acknowledge the powers of the universe when you express and feel gratitude. Feeling grateful will bring peace and serenity into your life. It will help to empower you!

Remember:
1. We create our own happiness by attracting it.
2. We feel happiness by acting happy, or acting as if we were happy.
3. We create our health by reducing stress and attracting peace and attracting health.
4. We create our mission in life.
5. We create our future by envisioning and believing it!
6. We create our personal wealth by imagining, planning, believing and acting!
7. We imagine and create our lives!
8. Anything we can imagine, we can achieve!
9. The power of *The Secret* is awesome!
10. Life is awesome!
11. We are awesome!

Section Four

What Could Hold Us Back or Encourage Breakdowns?

What could really prevent us from achieving our dreams? Why would we experience breakdowns that hold us back? There are several reasons:

1. If we don't have a clear Vision. A clear vision gives us purpose, clarity and direction. Otherwise we get confused and diffused! We get confused about what we may want and loose our focus. If we don't have a clear destination and no clear directions, we won't reach our dreams. Our dreams will remain only dreams. For our dream to become reality, our true desire or objective MUST be *written down* and *visualized!* Looking at photos, graphics and written declarations daily become vivid reminders that propel us toward our dreams each day! We must focus on what we want!

2. If we don't have Motivation or don't understand what it is. If we don't know why we want something, we won't be motivated to achieve it. Our personal motivation is the fuel in the engine that drives us! Motivation propels us! Motivation creates passion! Our motivation is the feeling we know we will have when we get something. The feeling we will have when we give to our favorite charity. The feeling when we help our family financially. The feeling when we drive our BMW or Porsche. The feeling of financial security. The feeling of being number one. The feeling of helping others. The promise of wonderful feelings determines our "Why we want something"—our true Motivations.

3. If we don't Ask. Asking the universe or a higher power for help and knowing that it will come has been a critical aspect of prayer and meditation in virtually every belief system for thousands of years. Why? Because it works! If you don't ask, you won't receive.

The Secret Agent—The Secret Daily System for Amazing Success

4. If we don't Believe. We must have faith in the universe or in some higher power and in ourselves. Our belief in getting what we ask for must be 100%! 95% is just not good enough. Self-doubt is nothing more than self-sabotage. Negativity kills dreams. Even a small amount of doubt and negativity will very likely limit any success. A huge doubt is like sticking a knife in an inflated beach ball—our dream will deflate instantly. A very slight doubt is like sticking a small pin in the beach ball—our dream will deflate very slowly over a period of time. Either way—our dream is doomed!

5. If we don't live in Gratitude. Expressing gratitude to the universe or a higher power keeps us positive, appreciative and helps to eliminate the stresses in life. We must be grateful for our lives—past, present and future.

6. If we don't take Action. If we don't take actions toward our goals daily, we simply won't accomplish much. It's terrific to dream. It takes actions to achieve our dreams. Our actions will translate our dreams into reality.

7. If we don't use a Daily System. A system gives us the essential structure to keep us on a path toward our target. Otherwise, it will be hit or miss—zig and zag—and we will wander aimlessly toward some of our goals. If we want to achieve our dreams fast, we need to use a fun and effective daily system for envisioning, planning and action!

Section Five

How You Get Your Big Mo Magic Going!
--Follow the System with Fun Daily Action Steps

Now it's time to take the powerful personal system you have developed to empower you in the weeks and months ahead, and customize it to one specific desire you want to attract into your life, and put that into a simple, brief daily system. If you take just one shot—one attempt at almost anything, it seldom succeeds. Your actions need to follow your visions—follow your plan. And you need to be *consistent* and *persistent!* You need to develop *The BIG MO! MOMENTUM!* There is a real magic in the power of momentum. When you develop *YOUR BIG MO*—you will become unstoppable!!! So, let's get *YOUR BIG MO MAGIC going!*

Take a moment to think. Take one specific thing that you really want to attract and go through the following sequence several times and notice how you feel. Keep it short. Keep it simple.

Verbalize out loud your responses to each question below. Take the time to visualize and believe. Start now!

- What specifically do I really want?

- Why do I really want it?

- How will getting it make me feel?

- How can I get it?

- How will I get it?

- Briefly, what is my strategy! (write it down and read it out loud daily)

- Briefly, what is my action plan! (write it down and read it out loud daily)

- What will I do each day to achieve it?

- Why will I act each day to achieve it?

- What about achieving it is important to me?

- I believe I will attain it! I know I am attaining it!

- I visualize myself attaining it! (take a moment now)

- What actions will I accomplish today?

- I visualize doing it! (take a moment now)

- I believe I will do it!

- I visualize having attained it! (take a moment now)

- How do I feel having attained it!

- I feel wonderful! I feel awesome!

- I enjoy the feeling!

This is a process that may be done with everything you wish to attract into your life. It only takes a few minutes each morning. This process will empower you. It is a process that will take you through the steps of implementing the powers of *The Secret—The Law of Attraction*. Remember the basic steps:

1. Ask—for what you want
2. Believe—that you will attract it
3. Visualize—it as if it has happened
4. Receive it—feel the way you will when it arrives
5. Act—look for opportunities and seize them
6. Be Grateful!

Also remember to:

- Be BOLD! Live LARGE!
- Live Your Big Dreams Daily!
- Empower yourself and share with others!
- Be open to change and opportunities.
- Be open to the energy of the universe.
- Commit to your Visions
- Decide to do it!
- Take Action! Just do it!!!!
- Live with Passion! Live with Joy!
- Celebrate you accomplishments each day!

Section Six

A Summary of the Important Steps to Attract Your Success and Happiness

The *Secret* is the Law of Attraction: We attract into our lives that which we think about, envision and firmly believe.

This has been proven again and again throughout history. And, we accomplish that which we act upon.

*First: ASK:
Ask for *what you want* in a voice as if you have already received it.
Ask for something you are passionate about. Write it and say it.
Examples:
"I am so happy and grateful now that I have made over $500,000 in income."
"I am so happy and grateful now that I have acquired a terrific $5 million dollar buyer."
"I am so happy and grateful now that I have acquired a terrific $5 million dollar seller."

*Second: BELIEVE:
Believe that it will happen and the universe will attract it. Have faith!
Believe it by *visualizing* and *feeling* the end result. Know it will happen. Trust the universe.
Repeat daily incantations.
Examples:
"What I desire, I attract"
"Money comes to me easily and frequently."
"I find a way daily to get what I want! I go to it and it comes to me!"
"Each day, in every way, I love getting stronger!"
"What I desire, I attract, and it make me feel fantastic!"

*Third: VISUALIZE:
Create your personal Vision Book right here in Section Seven of this action book. Use photos and cutouts and look at them daily. Focus on what you want! Take a few moments daily. Visualize it, picture it vividly, think it, feel it as if it has already happened and believe it daily!

*Fourth: RECEIVE:
Be ready to receive what you want. Feel the way you will once it arrives. Step into you successful future. You deserve it! Feel it! Enjoy it!

*Fifth: ACT!
Look for opportunities. Awaken to recognize opportunities. Seize opportunities daily! Time is of the essence daily. Step into your visions! Make decisions to act! Take action! Achieve each commitment you make. Just do it! Take productive action!

*Sixth: Live each day in GRATITUDE:
Develop an attitude of gratitude. Begin each day by being grateful!
Create a list daily of what you are grateful for in your life.

Repeat incantations of gratitude.
Examples:
"I am so grateful for…"
"I love my life!"
"I love myself."
"I love my opportunities!"
" I am so grateful for…"

Create a list daily of what you *will be* grateful for.
Repeat incantations of gratitude as if you have already received it.
Examples:
"I am so grateful now that…"
"I am so grateful now that…"
"I am so grateful now that…"

Remember:
1) We create our own happiness by attracting it.
2) We create our health by reducing stress and attracting peace and attracting health.
3) We create and make our mission in life.
4) We create our future by envisioning and believing it!
5) We create our personal wealth by imagining, planning, believing and acting!

Ask yourself:

- What specifically do I really want?

The Secret Agent—The Secret Daily System for Amazing Success

- Why do I really want it?
- How will getting it make me feel?
- How can I get it?
- How will I get it?
- Write the strategy!
- Write the action plan!
- What will I do each day to achieve it?
- Why will I act each day to achieve?
- What about achieving it is important to me?
- Believe in attaining it!
- Visualize having attained it!
- What actions will I accomplish today?
- Visualize doing it!
- Believe you will do it!
- Empower yourself and share with others!
- Be open to opportunities!
- Be open to the energy of the universe!
- Commit and decide to do it!
- Just do it!!!!
- Get excited! Enjoy it!
- Celebrate your accomplishments each day!
- Rock your wonderful world! Enjoy life!
- Life is truly amazing!

Section Seven

My Personal Vision Book

I see it in my life. I feel it in my life. I will attract:

My Personal Vision Book

I see it in my life. I feel it in my life. I will attract:

My Personal Vision Book

I see it in my life. I feel it in my life. I will attract:

My Personal Vision Book

I see it in my life. I feel it in my life. I will attract:

My Personal Vision Book

I see it in my life. I feel it in my life. I will attract:

My Personal Vision Book

I see it in my life. I feel it in my life. I will attract:

My Personal Vision Book

I see it in my life. I feel it in my life. I will attract:

My Personal Vision Book

I see it in my life. I feel it in my life. I will attract:

My Personal Vision Book

I see it in my life. I feel it in my life. I will attract:

My Personal Vision Book

I see it in my life. I feel it in my life. I will attract:

My Personal Vision Book

I see it in my life. I feel it in my life. I will attract:

Section Eight

A Framework for Focus—*Your 3-3-3-3 Focus System*
A Framework for Your Yearly, Monthly and Weekly Business Plans

A Framework for Focus:

Light beams can be weak, diffused and scattered, or they can be focused into a powerful laser beam. We all need to *focus* to become *powerful* as well. Here is a powerful ***3-3-3-3 Focus System*** to power your focus and focus your personal power.

- Focus on one Big Vision
- Focus on three Strategies to achieve it
- Focus on three Actions for each strategy
- Consider three potential Challenges to achieving the strategies
- Focus on three Corrective Actions to overcome the challenges

Now it's time to go through this focus process with one of your Big Visions. To focus on one achievement at a time, ask yourself the questions on the following two pages and write in the answers. Before doing so, you may wish to run a few copies of the 3-3-3-3 Focus System on the next pages.

This is fun and highly effective. This system will help you attract your Big Vision! This is fun! Let's get started!

My 3-3-3-3 Focus System

- What will I now focus on achieving or attracting into my life?

My Big Vision is _____

_____

_____

_____

_____

- What are three good **Strategies** to achieve it?

1. _____
2. _____
3. _____

- What are three **Action** steps I will take to accomplish **#1 Strategy** above?

1. _____
2. _____
3. _____

- What are three **Action** steps I will take to accomplish **#2 Strategy** above?

1. _____
2. _____
3. _____

- What are three **Action** steps I will take to accomplish **#3 Strategy** above?

    1. _____
    2. _____
    3. _____

- What three **Challenges** might prevent me from achieving each of the three **Strategies** above?

    1. _____
    2. _____
    3. _____

- What three **Corrective Actions** will I take to overcome these **Challenges**?

    1. _____
    2. _____
    3. _____

Now:

Visualize it! -- Visualize your Big Vision daily

Believe it! -- Believe you will attract it daily!

Do it daily! -- Take your committed Actions daily!

Receive it! -- Accept opportunities, receive and rejoice daily!

A Framework for Your Yearly, Monthly and Weekly Business Plan:

How many things do we think about each day? Studies have shown that on most occasions we sort through over 10,000 thoughts and messages per day. Some experts say the number of impulses our brains process is over 50,000. Amazing!

How many things do we do each day? Studies have show that we take hundreds of actions each day. Understandable. We are busy 24-7. Even when we are sleeping our minds and bodies are busy.

We cram the demands of work, play, family, friends, exercising, eating, sleeping, cleansing, driving, recreation, reading, learning, relaxing, etc. into our lives virtually every day. No wonder we sometime have a tendency to feel overwhelmed. It is so easy to have great intentions, but to let them slip away as our time slips away.

Many of us have the tendency to want to accomplish too many things in too short a period of time. It's just human nature in a hectic world. And by putting pressure on ourselves to try to accomplish too many things each day, we often set ourselves up for a *feeling of failure*. Not necessarily failure, but the *feeling* of failure.

For example, if we place pressure upon ourselves to accomplish thirty things in one day and at the end of our day, we see that we only accomplished five of them, we may likely feel as if we had a bad day. But if we focused on accomplishing the five most important, most impactful things that day and we accomplished them, and if the other twenty-five things were not really important to get done that day, then we should feel wonderful! If those five things we accomplished brought us much closer to achieving our Big Vision—Our Dream—then we had a fantastic day!

This shows the tremendous importance of prioritization and focus! Studies have shown that approximately 20% of our actions result in approximately 80% of our big achievements. It's the old *80/20 Rule* again.

The easiest and most effective ways to fight against feelings of overwhelm and failure are to prioritize and focus daily. This is also the way you effectively

The Secret Agent—The Secret Daily System for Amazing Success

implement the principles of *The Secret*. Remember: What you focus on is what you will attract into your life. And to take it one step further: What you make a priority and take action on is what you will accomplish.

The way to become highly effective on a daily, weekly and monthly basis is to ask yourself:

1. What are the *most important* 2 or 3 things I will accomplish today? **Without fail!!!** Meaning, no matter what happens, I will find a way to accomplish these 2 or 3 things today! **Absolutely without fail!!!**
2. What are the *most important* 2 or 3 things I will accomplish this week? **Without fail!!!** Meaning, no matter what happens, I will find a way to accomplish these 2 or 3 things this week! **Absolutely without fail!!!**
3. What are the *most important* 2 or 3 things I will accomplish this month? **Without fail!!!** Meaning, no matter what happens, I will find a way to accomplish these 2 or 3 things this month! **Absolutely without fail!!!**

Most of us have a lot more than 2 or 3 things on our to-do lists each day and week and month. But to become most powerful and effective, we need to ***prioritize, then focus, then act! We need to focus on Our Biggies!***

We may let other, less important things fall by the wayside each day, but we must not let the 2 or 3 most important things slip. These 2 or 3 most important objectives—Our Biggies—must be accomplished without fail as if a matter of life and death. No excuses, no rationalizations!

Can you just imagine how powerful and effective you daily life would be if you did this each day? Without fail! And, can you just imagine how wonderful and powerful you would feel at the end of each day if you accomplished your 2 or 3 most important objectives to move closer to the achievement of one of your Big Visions—Big Dreams? You would feel incredible! You would feel amazing! Can you imagine how successful and happy you would be if you focused on and accomplished just three significant priorities each active day over the course of a year? That would be between 750 and 1,000 powerful accomplishments each year! Your life would be amazing!

Always remember: Handle your daily, weekly and monthly Biggies—and you will Live Large! You will achieve your Big Visions and your Big Dreams!

So, why not start doing it on a daily basis right now? *Bring passion to each day!* Let's go!

My Unstoppable Priorities –- My Points of Focus — My Biggies:

This month, I *will* accomplish, absolutely without fail, the following Biggies:

1. _____
2. _____
3. _____

This week, I *will* accomplish, absolutely without fail, the following Biggies:

1. _____
2. _____
3. _____

Today, I *will* accomplish, absolutely without fail, the following Biggies:

1. _____
2. _____
3. _____

Brighten you life! Live *The Secret* and Beyond today…and every day! Attract your success and happiness!

Section Nine

My Daily Vision Sheets

My Top Three Motivators or Motivations:

1. _____
   _____

2. _____
   _____

3. _____
   _____

My Big Vision #1:

_____
_____
_____

My Big Vision #2:

_____
_____
_____

My Big Vision #3:

_____
_____
_____

Visualize Achieving Them! Visualize and Feel As If You Have Achieved Each!

My Unstoppable Priorities – My Points of Focus – My Biggies:

This month, I *will* accomplish, absolutely without fail, the following Biggies:

1. _____
2. _____
3. _____

This week, I *will* accomplish, absolutely without fail, the following Biggies:

1. _____
2. _____
3. _____

Today, I *will* accomplish, absolutely without fail, the following Biggies:

1. _____
2. _____
3. _____

I Visualize –

I Believe –

I Act –

I Receive!

I Enjoy!

The Secret Agent—The Secret Daily System for Amazing Success

My Gratitude List

Repeat incantations of gratitude.

Examples: "I am so grateful for…" "I love my life!" "I love myself." "I love my opportunities!" "We live in a world of opportunities!" "I am so grateful for…"

Make your gratitude list. Write it now! Read it out loud every morning!

1. _____

2. _____

3. _____

4. _____

5. _____

6. _____

7. _____

8. _____

9. _____

10. _____

Remember to:
- Empower yourself and share with others!
- Be open to change and opportunities.
- Be open to the amazing energy of the universe.
- Commit to it and decide to do it!
- Just do it!!!!
- Live with passion!
- Celebrate your accomplishments each day!
- Be **BOLD!** Live LARGE!
- Live Your Big Dreams Daily!

I Visualize –

I Believe –

I Act –

I Receive!

I Enjoy!

☺

The Secret Agent—The Secret Daily System for Amazing Success

About the Author

Ralph Merritt Nedelkoff received an undergraduate degree from the University of Notre Dame and a master's degree in management from The American University in Washington, DC. He has over 20 years of successful management experience in the residential real estate business on both the East Coast and the West Coast. After a successful 6-year career in real estate sales and marketing, Ralph served as a top manager, trainer and coach with real estate companies within several national franchises: Better Homes & Gardens, The Prudential, GMAC, Keller Williams and Coldwell Banker. He also trained agents involved in five of the top luxury marketing affiliation in the United States: Sotheby's International, GMAC Elegant Homes, Better Homes & Gardens Elegant Homes, Prudential Fine Homes and Coldwell Banker Previews.

Ralph is currently conducting inspiring personal training, tele-training, coaching, consulting, speaking and luxury specialty certifications—as well as providing valuable tools to assure your success in the luxury field—all through his website. Be sure to visit: **www.TheWorldOfLuxuryRealEstate.com**

Ralph is also the author of several more books for your business:

- ***The World of Luxury Real Estate – 2008 Edition—The Ultimate Training Guide for Real Estate Agents*** – How to Seize the Amazing Opportunities in Today's $200 Billion Luxury Real Estate Market. Plus Inside Tips and Interviews with 25 of the Top Luxury Superstars in the World! Available from Amazon.com and TheWorldOfLuxuryRealEstate.com

- ***Go Wild Today! Passions into Actions! –The Ultimate Daily Motivational System for Real Estate Professionals*** – Get motivated and stay motivated daily! Plug into this simple yet amazing motivational system. This is the book that gets it done daily! Available at Amazon.com

- ***The Secret Superstar*** – The Secret Daily System for Amazing Success. A must for All Sales Professionals. Available at Amazon.com

- ***The Secret Entrepreneur*** – The Secret Daily System for Amazing Success. A must for All Entrepreneurs. Available at Amazon.com

Ralph is also the author of two works of fiction for your enjoyment:

- ***Ruler of Men – The Amazing Lady at 1600 Penn*** – An inspirational novel about the first female President. She's not your ordinary President. And she just happens to be a Democrat, but it's not Hillary! Was she part of the most dramatic international conspiracy in history? This book is available at Amazon.com

- ***The Ecstasy of Moonbeams, The Magic of Light*** – A book of poetic inspirations and glimpses into the awesome powers and mysteries of our amazing universe, and the universe within ourselves. It is also available at Amazon.com

For additional terrific information be sure to visit our website:
www.The-Secret-Agent.net

Be BOLD!

Live LARGE!

Live Your Big Dreams Daily!

☺

Made in the USA
Middletown, DE
03 January 2015